GRIEF IN
YOUNG
CHILDREN

GRIEF IN YOUNG CHILDREN

A HANDBOOK FOR ADULTS

ATLE DYREGROV

Jessica Kingsley Publishers
London and Philadelphia

First published in 2008
by Jessica Kingsley Publishers
116 Pentonville Road
London N1 9JB, UK
and
400 Market Street, Suite 400
Philadelphia, PA 19106, USA

www.jkp.com

Library of Congress Cataloging in Publication Data

Dyregrov, Atle.
  Grief in young children : a handbook for adults / Atle Dyregrov.
    p. cm.
  ISBN 978-1-84310-650-0 (pb : alk. paper) 1. Grief in children. 2. Children and death. I.
Title.
  BF723.G75D975 2008
  155.9'370833--dc22
                2007040140

British Library Cataloguing in Publication Data
A CIP catalogue record for this book is available from the British Library

ISBN 978 1 84310 650 0

Printed and bound in Great Britain by
Athenaeum Press, Gateshead, Tyne and Wear

Thank you to all the children
and parents who have taught
me so much over the years

Contents

Foreword

For much of the last century, many adults acted as if young children should be seen but not heard. The children did not know this – they both saw and heard, often what adults were mistakenly trying to protect them from. Thus, while bereaved adults comforted themselves with the thought that children could not understand death and dying, the children were often abandoned to a great sense of confusion.

Not content with writing one of the best books on grief in children, Atle Dyregrov has now penned this sensitive and accessible account of how preschool children react to death – and, as importantly, how parents can help them adjust to changes in family life. The text is full of poignant examples of how very young children understand and misunderstand what has happened and also has clear advice as to how adults should actively listen to them and support them.

The issues of whether young children should see the dead body and should participate in funeral rituals are dealt with head on – in most circumstances they should. Seeing the dead body of a loved one – after careful preparation for what they will see – helps even the youngest child realize that death is the end of life. Participating in rites they may not fully understand at the time can be comforting in later years.

This insightful text will be of great help to all who care for preschool children – parents, kindergarten teachers, ministers of religion, police, welfare workers – the list is endless. If they learn the values reflected in this small book, then bereaved children everywhere will grow up with far fewer hang-ups about the only certainty in life.

William Yule
Emeritus Professor of Applied Child Psychology,
Institute of Psychiatry, King's College London; and Chair,
Children and War Foundation
November 2007

Chapter One

What is grief?

———◆———

Children can experience many kinds of loss. They can lose their mother, father, sister or brother through death, or they can lose daily contact with one or several loved ones through divorce, being placed in a foster home or through adoption. The most common loss children experience, however, is the death of their grandmother or grandfather. This can be extremely painful because they have often played an important part in the child's everyday life. But children can also experience loss when a friend becomes ill or dies, when they themselves or someone they care about moves far away, or when a pet dies. All these losses can trigger grief in children. Some children are taken away from parents who are unable to take care of them. Others have an illness or injury which means they have to amputate or lose the use of a limb, with the sense of loss and grief that this can cause.

We do not need to go back many years to the time when it was doubted that children were able to grieve. Particularly questionable was whether young children could grieve. Fortunately this notion now belongs to the past, and we are now asking ourselves how children grieve and how parents can understand children's grief. The aim of this book is primarily dealing with children's grief after someone they care about has died. Many of the reactions described and the measures suggested will, all the same, also be useful if the child's grief has been triggered by other losses.

What understanding do young children have of death?

The term 'young children' covers the age range from birth to starting school age. The way death is understood will vary enormously between tiny babies and children who are ready to start school. In order to understand death, a child must have developed concepts which enable him to grasp what has happened when someone has died. Children between the ages of two and two and a half have only a slight understanding of what death is, and children aged under two are usually too young to be able to grasp this at all. Between four and six years of age the child gradually develops a biological more than a psychological understanding of what life is and that life depends on the function of the body's organs. As children approach school age they can understand that the body's organs have the task of sustaining life. This biological understanding is a prerequisite for understanding that if any of the organs fail or are damaged, we may die. Young children seldom understand death in the way an adult does, but as they approach school age, more biological understanding of the body and their increased cognitive maturity enable them to understand more of what has happened.

Children find it difficult to understand that death is universal. They will have to grasp that all life must end at some time or another, including themselves. They have to understand that death is final, that the dead person cannot come back. Children have to understand that all bodily functions cease, which means that the dead person can no longer breathe, eat, go out and play, and that he or she cannot think, feel or dream. They also have to understand the reasons why we die. They have to learn to differentiate between 'magic' causes, like someone wishing that a person would die and then they do, and the real causes of death. Children will gradually come to understand that death is not only caused by external circumstances, such as being shot for example, but it can also be caused by illness or old age. The preschool child finds it easier to imagine death being caused by accidents or weapons rather than old age or illness. In a similar way, the loss experienced through divorce is connected more to quarrels and conflicts than the parents' discontent with their relationship as a couple.

Many young children show through their questions and comments that they have not developed a deeper understanding of what death is:

'Daddy's coming back after the summer holiday, isn't he?'

'Mummy's been away for so long. When's she coming back?'

It is easy to think that this is just a matter of children not having the capacity to understand, and we forget that a child will seldom have lived long enough to have gained his or her own experiences of death, which enable them to develop insight into it.

As children lack a concrete understanding of what has happened, they may demand to be taken to visit the dead person at the place they are at now, or they may insist that the dead person will come back in a similar way to their experience of someone going to work or being away for a few days. Children find it difficult to understand that death is final. They are used to things being repeated: that they get up each morning, go to kindergarten, come home and the next day it all happens again. Everything happens again, so why shouldn't the person who has gone come back again? Their perception of time only gradually becomes more like an adult's, with a line running from the past, through the present and into the future.

The understanding of a very young child (under three years of age) becomes apparent in simple statements which confirm that what children experience is the absence of someone who is normally present in their daily life: 'Daddy dead, Daddy gone. Daddy dead, Daddy gone. Mummy's here.' Gradually, as a child realizes that the dead person is not coming back, he or she will understand that death is final. Their concrete understanding is reflected in their questions:

'Who will give him food down in his grave?'

'Who will cut Grete's hair now?'

Some children have only heard of death taking place in a violent way, whether they have seen this on television or heard about it from friends at kindergarten, and their understanding of the cause of death is along these lines. 'Who shot him?' may be the question asked by a five-year-old when his friend tells him that his grandfather has died.

Children under two years of age are able to notice the absence of someone who has usually been there, and can go to their bed, point and say 'Ba' or 'Mamma' or point at a picture and say 'where?' Although children under two years old usually will have a scant understanding of death, some children understand much even at this age:

A girl around two years of age, already with an advanced vocabulary, asked her mother questions about her father's suicide much ahead of her age. The mother had asked professionals for advice and they all said the same: she is too young to understand death. I held the same notion when she asked me after a speech I gave on children and death. The mother called me six months later when the girl was two and a half years old and said that the girl now asked why the father had done what he did and other advanced questions for her age. My advice was then to answer her as truthfully as she could. If the child was old enough to ask such direct and relevant questions, she apparently understood more than we could fathom and was advanced enough to be met at her own level and have her experience acknowledged.

A three-year-old can sometimes formulate questions and comments which show that they have a more highly developed understanding of death than adults realize:

Lisa was sitting with her playmate (both aged between three and four) and they were talking about how unfair it is that some young people die before they are old.

A four-year-old who is given proper information and the opportunity to ask questions can understand a good deal of the implications of death:

Stian lost his best friend in an accident. He didn't understand what had happened and kept asking when his friend was coming back. After he had been and seen his friend in the coffin, he sat in the car and said: 'Now we'll never be able to play in the sandpit any more. Now we can't play on the swings any more.'

This concrete meeting with death meant that the child was able to take a big leap forward in his understanding of what death was, and he was able to formulate this in his own words. Sometimes it is the child's limited experience that limits their understanding and that can make adults smile in the midst of grief:

A boy of four was present at his grandparent's funeral. The family was gathered around the grave and the priest was saying the words 'earth to earth, ashes to ashes' as he used his small spade to put some earth on the coffin. The boy saw the large pile of earth, looked at the priest and then at his mother before he stated: 'This is going to take a long time.'

During their preschool years and particularly during their first years of school, children gradually understand that death is irrevocable and that all the bodily functions cease. After a while they also understand that death is unavoidable and everyone, including themselves, will die one day. Children who have lost someone who has been dear to them have a greater understanding of the different aspects of death than their peers who have not experienced a loss of this kind. Occasionally, personal experiences can cause anxiety, which is an obstacle to understanding, as a good deal of the child's mental capacity is 'locked up' in watching out for new dangers.

Often, children have taken in more than adults understand:

> Three-year-old Cecilia lost her elder brother in an accident. She accompanied her parents to my office and as they told their story she made a drawing containing details from the accident that shows she must have heard what happened. She must have had 'big ears' when her parents had told others who came to visit, or overheard telephone conversations. When the parents saw the drawing, it was not hard for them to understand that they had to spend more time talking directly with Cecilia.

Children of preschool age gain a broader understanding of death through the concrete facts they pick up from the information they are given by parents and other adults, for example by looking at photograph albums or video films, or by going to visit the grave itself. A child who experiences a loss at the age of three may have a different understanding of this loss when he or she is six and a half. The child may then go back to what happened with questions and comments which show that they have greater insight into what has happened, and can seek out information which can help them understand better the events that took place when they were younger.

It is important for adults to listen actively to the child so that they can understand the child's understanding of death, ask careful questions which help to reveal what the child may not understand and be sensitive to the themes that may be behind the child's questions.

Many people do not talk to preschool children about divorce, thinking that they do not react much to it. If children continue living in the same home, it may be difficult for them to realize and understand the changes they notice, and they may become slightly confused. The explanation that their parents are no longer going to live together, and a clear message about how visits to the parent who is no longer living with them will take place, prevent confusion.

How do young children react to loss?

Immediate reactions

The range of children's reactions is very great. When they hear that someone has died, or that their parents are going to get divorced, reactions can vary from no reaction at all to strong emotional outbursts. Some protest loudly: they shout and cry and want to strike out in anger against the parent who is relating what has happened. Others seem not to have taken in what has been said, and the parents start telling them again because they think the child has not heard what was said. It is not unusual for preschool children not to react, but many parents find this surprising. Straight after having been told what has happened, a child may ask if he or she can go out to play. This kind of reaction may be a sign that the child is pushing thoughts about what has happened to one side, so that they can take them in a little at a time. But this may also reflect the fact that young children are seldom able to grasp the long-term consequences of what has happened until they gradually come to understand that the person who has gone is not coming back.

If parents are going to be divorced, young children can be given the chance to see the house their mummy or daddy is going to live in. Information, visits and explanations about the concrete changes separation or divorce bring about will help to calm the child's thoughts.

Some children will be so shocked by the news that someone they love is dead or dying, or that they are going to move, that they are unable to speak and remain sitting in apathy, unable to react. Some preschool children who have been present when their mother or father died or was killed have stayed sitting by the bed or at the scene of the death for a long time, doing nothing, sometimes remaining silent for many days afterwards. When the message a child receives does not bring about an immediate alteration in their everyday life, for example if one of his parents has been diag-nosed as having a fatal disease or his parents are going to be divorced, the child may not show any particular reaction until he notices things changing in the home, such as Mummy not being there any more or not being able to do as much as before.

So, immediate reactions can vary from protest to crying, anger or apathy. Adults are acting wisely if they refrain from pressing the child to react in a particular way and instead accept and confirm the child's reaction: 'I can understand that you are angry. It's awful that this has happened. Mummy is also cross, but she's also very sad that your little sister is dead' or 'It is strange that Daddy is not here and I know that you, as I, expect him to come home from work as usual, but he will not. When someone is dead he is gone for ever, but you can always keep him inside and see him in front of you as he was.'

Common secondary reactions

We can divide secondary reactions into those which present themselves in the first days and weeks after a death, and those which may extend over months and years. The reactions described here are normal reactions to death. Many, but by no means all, children have one or several of these reactions, and there is great variation in their type, intensity and duration. As many children only gradually realize what has happened, through the absence of the person they have lost, it is perhaps the most normal for there to be an absence of reaction first of all. The youngest children need repetition of the fact that the dead person has gone and will not come back again. In this way, they come to understand that the loss is real. However, other common reactions are:

- anxiety and fear, including separation anxiety
- sleep disturbances
- anger and attention-demanding behaviour
- withdrawal and isolation
- sadness, longing and loss
- guilt and self-condemnation
- play connected to what has happened
- thoughts about meaning
- more childish behaviour
- distressing reliving of events and disturbing fantasies.

Anxiety, fear and separation anxiety

When someone important in a child's daily life dies and disappears, they become afraid that this will happen to others too. Young children show that they are afraid by constantly demanding the presence of their parents or the surviving parent:

> Ken became almost desperate when he couldn't see us. He insisted on having the door to the landing open at night, he always wanted the light to be on and he kept calling out to reassure himself that we were there.

This example is fairly typical. Young children show their fear in their need to be near their parents as well as a great need for physical closeness with their parents, which some parents find clinging. The very youngest children are less eager to wander away from their parents when they are exploring their surroundings, and they are quick to crawl back to their mother or father if something unexpected happens.

Such separation anxiety can be very tiresome for parents and they sometimes need concrete advice from health professionals on how it may be alleviated:

> Following his wife's death in childbirth a father was left alone with a girl of four who wanted to know of his whereabouts at all times. He noticed how he had to be very careful about telling her where he was, and at bedtime he had to repeat where he could be found if she woke up. He also said that it is much easier if his daughter walks further away from him than the other way round. The child needed to have full control of her 'security base', her father, and due to his sensitive and gradual approach to separation she achieved more control and can better tolerate distance.

Children may also cling to teddy bears, comforters and so on, which make them feel secure, and they clearly can become more nervous, complaining, clinging or have temper tantrums. Six- to seven-year-olds can express verbally that they are afraid something is going to happen to their parents, but they may also be afraid that something is going to happen to themselves. This is also true for a number of younger children:

> Vegard was three years old when his younger sister died suddenly, less than 24 hours after his mother took her to hospital. After this he did not want to be near his mother, and he only let his father take care of him. He thought it was his mother's fault that his sister had died, since the last he saw of his sister was his mother hurrying out of the house with her. His fear that she would also go off with him and he would never be able to come back was tremendous and it was only after sensitive help from the hospital staff, where the boy was told how important it was that his mother had brought his sister to them, that his fear began to lessen.

If it is a friend who dies, children will realize that they can die, and they may become afraid of illness or accidents. Children are usually more afraid of losing their parents than that something may happen to themselves. If the question 'Can I die too?' arises, the child needs to be given both explanations of death and reassurances of her own safety. It is not unusual for a parent's death to trigger fear in children about what will happen to them:

> 'Who will buy food for me now?'

> 'Who will look after me if you die, Daddy?'

This existential fear can be met with a description of what is going to change and what will remain the same:

> 'Even though Daddy is dead, we will still go on living here. Mummy will fetch you from kindergarten each day and organize the food. Mummy will come a bit later to the

kindergarten to fetch you, because she has to finish work first. She'll come just after the fruit break.'

Children need information, reassurances, understanding of their reactions and needs, and the sense of security that life will continue more or less as before.

Sleep disturbances

Young children frequently react with sleep disturbances after a loss. They do not want to go to bed, and once they have gone to bed they are very restless so that it can take a long time before they fall asleep. The need to have the light on and the door open are indications of the anxiety which often keeps them awake because thoughts and fantasies enter into the conscious mind when there is nobody else there and they are not taking part in activities and play. They may also wake up more often at night and call out, cry, moan or talk in their sleep, probably as a result of bad dreams or nightmares. Unfortunately, some parents still use sleep as a way of explaining death: 'She's gone to sleep and won't wake up again.' Explanations like this make young children frightened to go to sleep themselves, and they also watch carefully over their parents taking a nap on the sofa or going to sleep in bed. They can also believe that if they make a lot of noise, the person will wake up again. Children create concrete and terrifying fantasies on the background of their parents' simple paraphrasing or images of death.

Anger and attention-demanding behaviour

Children can feel explosive anger when someone they love is no longer there. These are confusing and overwhelming feelings for young children, and their reactions may make them feel desperate, especially if they are coming up to school age:

Mark (aged six) lost his baby sister to sudden infant death syndrome (SIDS). He became angry and unmanageable, and even cruel to others in the kindergarten. After one of his temper tantrums he was sorry for what he had done. Advice from a school psychologist to his mother on how she could handle the anger, by being friendly but firm, and at the same time helping Mark to give words to the emotions gradually helped him to obtain more control over his anger. Parallel with this Mark's mother talked about the sister who had gone, that it was OK and that he did not have to be afraid if he saw that Mama was sad and cried.

Children commonly direct their anger at their parents or other people close to them, but they are seldom able to express it with such verbal clarity as this five-year-old: 'It's your fault. If you hadn't gone to the hospital with the baby, she wouldn't have died.' He kept hitting his mother as he said this. Children often become more difficult to deal with at kindergarten, and their anger affects other children. Sensitive and understanding adults who allow them to react, but help them to find ways of expressing their feelings without hurting other people, are an enormous help in this kind of situation.

Sometimes the anger may be directed at siblings, which may be very worrying for parents:

A five-year-old, who had lost his father, started hitting his newborn sister, and his mother was getting worried. The boy could not bear all the attention the baby was getting, especially as the father, who had looked after him while his mother took care of the baby, was no longer there. By behaving like this, he was able to draw his mother's attention to him. She arranged to get help with the baby, so that she could spend more time with the little boy.

Withdrawal and isolation

Some young children withdraw from other children in the aftermath of a loss, and they spend more time alone in the kindergarten or their home environment. These reactions are perhaps more usual in older children, but they can also be found in young children. In some cases this may be attributed to differences in their parents' mood and the kind of attention they get from them, which results in the children not being stimulated in the same way as before the loss. If this kind of reaction becomes apparent, adults should be aware that a child may be struggling with thoughts and feelings which they need help from an adult to express. Parents can help to counteract isolation by actively involving the child in relationships with other children.

Sadness, longing and loss

It is unusual for young children to show their grief by crying much. They have less tolerance for strong feelings than adults, and they will therefore try to keep what has happened at a distance. Children have a shorter span of sadness than adults and will not usually be sad for long periods of time. This does not mean that they do not continue to think about the person who has passed away for a long time, or that they do not miss and long for him or her. They may fantasize about where the lost person is now that real life no longer allows them to be together. This short span of sadness may lead adults to believe that children do not grieve as much and as deeply as they actually do:

> In the aftermath of his father's death a six-year-old said to his mother: 'Anyone who thinks this is sad, raise their hand.'

Children build bridges over their sense of loss by seeking out places where they have been together with the dead person, or they seek out situations and things they associate with the dead person. They may also find closeness and build bridges over their sense of loss by smelling the dead person's clothes, or looking at pictures, videos or things they have been given by the person who has passed away. But children also protect themselves by denying what has happened, either in their imagination or through their actions: 'Let's go and visit my little brother in hospital' or 'Is that you on the phone, Mummy?'

The oldest preschool children can sometimes have experiences of the dead person being in the same room as them, although this reaction is more common in older children.

Guilt and self-condemnation

Young children can easily think that things which happen are a result of their own thoughts or actions. This magical thinking means that they take an irrational responsibility for things that happen:

> Helen was seven years old when her mother suddenly died. In a conversation almost four years later, she was asked whether she remembered the circumstances around what had happened. She answered: 'Yes, I remember it well, and I remember I thought it was my fault because I hadn't tidied my room.'

Self-condemnation should particularly be looked out for in the case of a sibling dying, as jealousy between siblings is fairly common. Feelings of guilt may also represent real guilt, for example when a child had a part to play in what happened, such as a car accident which occurred because the child was disturbing the driver, or the six-year-old who persuaded his four-year-old brother out onto water with thin ice and the four-year-old drowned:

A 20-year-old woman sought help in early adult age and told how she had carried guilt feelings since she, as a three-year-old, was out of the home on the day that her younger sister became ill and died. She had always blamed herself for not being at home: 'If I had been at home it would not have happened.' This irrational guilt feeling had never been touched by adults and had grown strong and bothersome.

Play connected to what has happened

Young children often express thoughts about and reactions to what has happened through play. In play they are able to make a connection between the past and the present, and they tussle with what has happened in order to understand it better. Children are also able to express different feelings through play. They may pretend that they die at home and in the kindergarten, or they may play funerals and rising up from the dead:

A seven-year-old boy buried a bee in a matchbox next to his sister's grave and made it clear to his parents that it was not to be dug up again. After a few months, he dug it up again to see what had happened to the bee.

This boy wanted to find out and to understand what happens when we are dead. It may seem to adults that the games are repeated without much variation, but just as the child's questions about death are often repeated with slight variations, games can also have small variations which increase the child's insight. Through play, the child can repeat, explore and test out what has happened, understand particularly difficult moments, express the desire to be able to do something to help and so on. They may do this in the kindergarten or at home, for example playing with cars that crash after they have experienced a car accident:

Following a plane crash in which a preschool teacher was killed, the parents related at a parents' meeting that their children were acting out the accident at home. Plane crashes and funerals were a part of their play for a while and enabled a processing of the events. Remarkably enough, the children did not play these games in the kindergarten until the staff themselves had processed the event and were able to 'accept' this form of play.

It is not unusual for young children to add small ritual ceremonies which help them to express their feelings. They draw other children into the game, direct it and can approach what has happened in an indirect way.

Sometimes, especially after traumatic deaths, play takes on a somewhat repetitive character. The game is varied very little or not at all; in fact, the child reacts if someone tries to change the game, and the game gives no lasting relief of tension. After divorce, for example, preschool children may look for small things or objects they can put together endlessly, and this game clearly does not calm their inner disquiet or tension. In cases like these, professional help should be sought to get advice on how to give the child the best possible support.

Thoughts about meaning

A number of children think about different aspects of meaning in relation to the loss, including how unfair it is that this should happen to them. This is primarily the case with children who have reached school age, but even very young children can express profound thoughts about the meaning of life:

> Marianne, aged three and a half, was talking to her friend after her father had been killed in a tragic car accident and said: 'It's so unfair that Daddy died before Grandma.' This is

an advanced use of language and advanced thinking in a child who is not yet preschool age. One of the first days after the death, she developed a high temperature without any other symptoms. Then she shocked her mother so severely by what she said, that her mother telephoned the psychologist she was in contact with even though it was the middle of the night. What Marianne said was: 'Do you know why I am sick, Mummy?' 'No.' 'It's because Daddy died.'

More childish behaviour

Children may take a step backwards in their development. They may start wetting the bed at night or wetting themselves during the day even though they were dry before the loss. They may use more 'baby language', suck their thumbs, refuse to do things they had begun to master (like getting dressed, for example), insist that an adult sits by their bed while they are going to sleep, and so on. This sort of behaviour is usually temporary, and if parents can be a little patient, they will find that it passes by itself.

Distressing reliving of events and disturbing fantasies

Sometimes children witness an incident of death and are left with a strong sensory impression of this event. This may be the case if a baby has suddenly died in the home or a child has died of asthma or something similar, or it may be that they survive an accident where others die, or the child may have witnessed acute illness in one of their parents, or found their mother or father dead as a result of illness, suicide or murder. Children can also receive strong impressions in the prelude to a loss through divorce, for example violence, threatening behaviour or verbal threats. In situations like these, the child takes in strong sensory impressions which may later return in the form of intrusive images and thoughts. In cases where the child was not present and hears about the event afterwards, he or she may develop bothersome fantasies about what happened which can become troubling.

Even children aged under two can have strong sensory memories; in other words, sensory impressions which live on in their memories and can later be put into words when the child masters language better. Things in children's everyday life may remind them of their loss and initiate reactions. They may react to a smell that reminds them of Daddy, or they may begin to cry when they hear music on the radio that was played at the funeral. These grief stimuli can be connected to sensory impressions or symbolic situations: 'Last time it was my birthday, I sat on Mummy's lap.' If the memories are connected to dramatic losses or situations, they are called 'traumatic reminders', like a car that looks like the one they were in when an accident took place, or the sea in the case of someone who has drowned:

> A girl of 17 explained that ever since she was two years old she has had bothersome recollections from a boating accident abroad, in which her mother died. She sees her mother lifeless, white in her face. She can clearly remember sitting on a stranger's lap, but nobody told her anything. When this happened she was too young to give words to it, and later it had been too strong for her to think about. She has tried to keep the memories at bay, but to no avail, and they have continued to bother her.

Long-term reactions

Although many of the reactions that have been described so far will subside during the first weeks and months after the loss, a sense of loss, longing and sadness can last for years, and to some extent for the rest of the child's life. This does not mean that the reactions will continue to be equally strong, but they can stay in the background of the child's life, especially if they have lost someone very close to them.

A very young child notices loss mostly through the changes in his daily routines; it is no longer Mummy who reads to him in the evening, it is Auntie who takes him to kindergarten, and so on:

> A six-year-old child would cry terribly every evening. She said that she missed her brother so much. He used to come in and give her a hug, but now he couldn't any more. She also thought about how he would have helped her with her homework when she started school, and he wouldn't be able to do that either.

There may be many things in children's everyday life that remind them about the person who is no longer there. These reminders can, with no warning, suddenly fill them with sadness and they may cry without always knowing why. Adults can help children to put words to this sense of loss and can comfort them when they are very upset.

If the death or loss happened suddenly, unexpectedly or in a particularly traumatic way, the event can potentially influence different aspects of the child's development. It is well known that traumatic events of this nature can alter a child's character and the shaping of their personality, their readiness to meet the future (reduced belief in the future), their ability to regulate strong feelings, their choice of career and their relationships with others (fear of losing those who are dear to them). As long as the children have caring adults and good care, there is little reason to expect that they will grow up with a greater risk of developing long-term psychological problems. It should be noted, however, that there is an increased risk of developing depression in children who lose parents in childhood.

Among the risk factors which increase the likelihood of a child having problems are:

- The child witnessed what happened (death, or violence before a divorce).

- The parents or the surviving parent develop or are already struggling with major problems (depression, post-traumatic disturbances and so on).

- The child experienced that he or she was in great danger.

- The child perceives strong reactions in the parent(s) without them being explained.

- The home circumstances are very negative for the child, with little warmth and friendly discipline (alcoholism, neglect).

- There is a high degree of denial of the events in the home, and a complete absence of open and direct talk about what has happened.

- There is development of serious behavioural disturbances or total change of personality.

During the preschool age, children learn to differentiate between different feeling states, something that continues during the primary school age, culminating in a deeper understanding of the origin of feelings and their conse-quences in adolescence. Traumatic situations will influence the tolerance for experiencing and differentiating feelings, interfering with the ability to feel compassion or empathy and expressing and tolerating strong feelings. Fear and anxiety can also lead to less exploration away from their security base (usually the mother or father) and children can become anx-iously attached, depending on the reliability of their parents. Learning to regulate feelings is totally dependent on adult care-takers. A child initiates interaction sequences, but adults must be sensitive and answer the child's signals for him or her to make use of this contact in their development and learning.

Small children are protected by their lack of ability to see the long-term consequences of a traumatic situation, and they understand danger to a lesser degree. As long as parents keep calm, young children can remain unconcerned. At the same time young children have less experience in interpreting an event, greater inclination for magical thinking and misunderstanding, and they are, to a lesser extent, able to reverse what happened in fantasy than older children. In addition, it is the younger children who are least included in conversations, who receive the least concrete information which can counteract fantasies, and are most easily overlooked following traumatic events. Such conditions makes it important to guide parents sensitively on how best to help their children.

Parents' reactions

Children's reactions to a loss will not only reflect their own grief and sense of loss, but also their parents' reactions to the loss. It is painful for a child to see his parents cry or find that his mother and father are not showing him the care they usually do. Parents who are suffering from grief will naturally have less energy to put into their children, and there are periods when parents can easily become impatient and annoyed when their children demand attention.

Many parents try to hide their reactions from their children in order to protect them. Our experience is that children are best served with parents who put their feelings into words so that they can better understand why their mother or father is reacting in the way he or she is. This also makes it easier for a child to show their own feelings and to share their thoughts with their parents.

If it is a child who has died it is very common for parents to become anxious about their other children. This often leads to overprotection or parents intervening in children's lives in other ways to ensure that nothing happens to them.

Health professionals in contact with the family can put these issues on the agenda during follow-up meetings with the parents or remaining parent, and they can provide advice that counteracts overprotection. Children's development is enhanced by:

- parents who can have their anxiety reduced

- parents who control their own anxiety at a distance

- parents who accept that the child gradually increases the distance from adults, and let others check on and provide feedback that their child is OK

- parents who refrain and manage their inclination to make sure that their child is safe at all times.

Chapter Two

What can be done to help children who have suffered a loss?

————

Early help for young children suffering grief

Below are some important guidelines for immediate help for children suffering from grief:

- Give them an immediate sense of being taken care of.

- Use physical closeness to provide security.

- Take the child onto your lap and relate what has happened, listen to the child's understanding of what you have said to make sure that they have grasped this, encourage them to express their thoughts and questions, and accept their reactions or lack of reaction.

- Place importance on giving the child information and facts about the loss which will contribute to a concrete understanding of the situation.

- Be careful to trace misunderstandings, misconceptions and magical thinking.

- Help the child find the personal meaning the events have for them.

- Set the scene so that the child can express what has happened in different ways; in other words, let the child talk, play or re-enact the events.

- Emphasize openness and honesty in the home.

- Return quickly to normal routines at home and in the kindergarten or school.

- As parents you will find advice about children's reactions and needs very helpful.

- Inform the kindergarten and/or school staff at an early stage so that they can give the child the best possible support.

It can be useful for even young children (from three to four years of age) to go through what has happened, as a help towards making their understanding as complete as possible and as a support for their memories at a later stage. This also helps children to clarify and counteract misunderstandings and prevents fantasies. Children need help to talk about this or express themselves in his or her own way. The parents or another caring adult can help the children to take part in a preliminary conversation and go over what has happened.

After a loss, children need security and structure around them. This can be achieved by the parents, or the surviving parent, maintaining the routines children are used to from their everyday life, such as mealtimes, bedtimes and so forth. When routines are maintained, they help to hold children's life together and provide a sense of security, for although the world has become insecure because of what has happened, there is still stability in many areas of their existence.

At an early stage after the event of loss, we can make sure that children are not creating fantasies based on a lack of understanding about what happened:

> Trond was four years old when he witnessed his brother being killed in a traffic accident. He saw his little brother get run over and tells in a conversation more than ten years later that he had thought they had taken his brother to hospital to put a tube into his mouth and blow air into him so that he would become 'big' again. He thought that he had become completely flat when he was run over and that he could be blown up in the same way as he had seen someone blowing up an air mattress.

This example shows how important it is not to take it for granted that the explanation and facts children are given are sufficient to ensure a correct understanding of events. We must make an active effort to grasp their understanding of the situation, an understanding which frequently differs considerably from what we had thought a child was thinking. We gain insight into the children's version through the questions they ask us, the drawings they make or by carefully asking them what they think about the events that have taken place.

If children are also prepared for their parents' reactions, they will be less inclined to take on the task of comforting them, pleasing them or protecting them. Children who see strong reactions in adults can easily become confused and think that it is something they have said or done that caused the reaction. From a very early age children react if somebody openly expresses sadness or is in pain. They will do their best to try to console. If parents explain why they are sad, for example after the death of a sibling, this can reduce the child taking on responsibility to better their parent's mood or getting them to laugh. If you give an explanation for why you are reacting as you do, this will relieve children's anxiety at the same time as they learn that it is all right to be unhappy or angry after something sad has happened. It is also exhausting for parents to go round pretending all the time, and in the long term this can make it hard to talk about difficult themes in the family.

What should children be told?

Whether a loss takes place suddenly or not, information and discussions with children will be of decisive significance for their ability to master what has happened. A number of parents use paraphrases when they tell their children about a loss. They might say that the dead person has gone to sleep, has passed away or that Daddy had to work somewhere else, is travelling and so forth. Sometimes people put off telling children what has happened or say that the person has been buried and will never come back. Many parents give what has happened a religious explanation: 'God wanted him because he was so good', 'She is with God now, so she's very happy', 'When we die, we'll go up to Jesus and live with great-grandfather'. Preschool children find it difficult to understand abstract explanations and may struggle with the idea that someone is down in the ground and up in heaven at the same time. They relate best to concrete explanations, and if you wish to give your child a religious explanation because of your own religion or convictions, you should use concrete images which make it easier for the child to understand. You can, for example, compare body and soul with a butterfly chrysalis. When the butterfly comes out and flies up in the sky, just the chrysalis shell is left.

Children often show a religious way of thinking, with concepts of the dead person living somewhere and being able to see them. They may have these thoughts quite independently of their parents' beliefs. If children have not been introduced to religious concepts (God, heaven) before, it is recommended that they be told concretely and directly what death means. A book by the Danish psychologist Anne Jacobsen (1989) describes directly and with great insight, what happens when we die, what happens during the funeral and burial/cremation, and what happens afterwards. Jacobsen (1989) even has pictures of a dead child and dead adults in her book.

To avoid a breakdown in trust between children and their parents, children must be given immediate and exact information. Allowing children to ask questions, giving them the answers we can and saying 'I don't know' when we do not know, helps children to grasp what has happened. Children have the same need as adults to make the loss real, and that takes place gradually. It may therefore be necessary to talk about what has happened over and over again.

When a child needs to be told about an incident of death, the following guidelines can be followed:

- Do not delay telling the child. If you feel 'shattered', you can wait until you have gathered your thoughts a little, or get help from another person your child trusts.

- Choose a place where there is peace and quiet to break the news, preferably a place the child is familiar with and feels secure in.

- Give direct, open and honest information in language appropriate to the child's age. Give the child the chance to prepare himself for what is coming, for example: 'I've something very sad to tell you. It's about Daddy. When he was on the train going to work today, the train crashed. Daddy hit his head very hard when this happened. Some doctors came to help him, but they couldn't save his life. He died in the ambulance on the way to the hospital because he was so damaged inside his head.' Although adults often want to paraphrase the truth or just tell parts of it, for example after suicide, it has been shown that openness is best. It strengthens the bond of trust between the child and the parent(s) as they grow up. Since young children have a concrete, but often incomplete understanding of what death is, you are recommended to follow up with concrete information: 'When we die, we stop breathing, our heart stops beating (let the child feel her own heart or your heart) and the person's hair and nails stop growing. Now that Daddy's dead, he can't feel any pain or anything, like if we pinch his hand, for example. He can't think any more either.'

- Sit with the child afterwards. Let them ask questions if they want to, but be aware of the fact that they may want to do something quite normal, such as going out to play, watching television, playing with Lego™ and so on, straight after they have heard the news.

- Reassure the child that you will still be there and that nothing is going to happen to you.

- As many children blame themselves for what has happened, whether it is death or divorce, it is important that the adult tells the child that it is nothing that they have done, thought or said that has caused what has happened.

Some losses are harder to tell children about than others. If their mother, father or a sibling has committed suicide, children are often given incorrect information or are not told the whole truth. These situations are a test of our ability to tell the truth. Children can be given the explanation that sometimes grown ups get an illness in their mind that makes them not want to live any more. They get so sad inside, much more than you or I do, so they make themselves die: 'Daddy took a pistol and shot himself with it so that he died.' It may seem brutal telling this to a preschool child, but if you can manage to be open right from the start, a sense of trust will be established which will be important in later childhood and adolescence. If the truth is not told, or only parts of it are told, children may later realize or hear the truth from others, and may be bitter and angry that the secret had been hidden from them. Younger children usually relate to 'strong' information in a level-headed and direct way, and may ask questions like: 'Where did it happen?', 'Can I look at the pistol?', 'Did he think about me?' and so on. It is mostly we adults who find being direct difficult, whereas children may take it quite naturally.

The Norwegian psychologist Magne Raundalen has provided a very useful 'recipe' on how parents (or a remaining parent) can tell and explain in a simple and direct way why some people take their own life. This explanation can be used for quite small children. If it is a parent that commits suicide, he explains it as an illness in the thoughts called 'depression' (not applicable in all situations). He then draws the thoughts as green and fresh long vertical lines, sometimes with flowers on. For thoughts to remain fresh and green the brain needs light and warmth. When one gets the disease named depression, it becomes dark and cold where the thoughts are, and they start to wither. If it becomes very cold and dark inside, the thought that we can go and get help also withers. Brown and black colours are used to illustrate the withering thoughts as leaves in autumn. The last thoughts that wither are the thoughts about our children, illustrated as green lines among the brown and dark ones. If these thoughts also grow ill, the person thinks: I cannot even take care of myself – how can I then be a father or mother to my children? Raundalen also describes concretely how the mode of death can be explained to children:

> Then there is only one thought left and it is ill. It is a dark thought inside the brain and it says: I must die. I must travel to death. That is the only place for me now. And to die one has to stop breathing and to stop breathing one has to put a rope around one's throat and that is called hanging. Or to end breathing I have to fill my lungs with water. That is called drowning. Or to die I have to tap out all my blood. That can be done by cutting one's pulse or putting a knife into one's heart. To die one has to stop the heart from beating and that can be done by very strong medicine. Or to die one has to take away all thoughts. That can be done by shooting a bullet into the brain. (Raundalen 2000 – translation by the author)

Depending on the way the suicide was committed an explanation is chosen.

Telling children that their mother and father are going to get divorced should follow the same principle. Open, honest and direct information, preferably given by the mother and father together, helps avoid upsetting children as far as possible. You should, to the extent that you can, also inform children what their everyday life will be like: where they will live, how often and how long they will stay with each of her parents and so on. At the same time, parents should tell their children that they can telephone Daddy or Mummy often if they miss them.

Avoid unnecessary separations between children and their parents

Some parents let others take care of their children when someone close has died because they feel they are unable to look after them well. This may increase the child's fear that their father and/or mother will disappear. If someone is to help parents with care of their children, it is therefore best if it can be done in familiar surroundings in the child's home. The sooner the mother or father can give closeness and contact to their child, the better. But this is something each individual has to feel for themself.

Chapter Three

Children's participation in rituals

———

Participation in rituals is important for children to learn about life and death. Rituals mark important events in a child's life, not only now but also in their future life. Being present at the funeral of a close family member is an opportunity the child will not get again, and this event can gain great symbolic meaning later in the child's life. This is one of the reasons that children's participation in rituals has been given such wide coverage in this book. Viewing the dead and the funeral help to make what has happened concrete and real. Participation in these rituals gives the child an important foundation for further understanding of what has happened. However, these rituals also prevent various fantasies of the type:

'Perhaps he isn't dead after all?'

'Perhaps there has been a mistake – it was someone else?'

Fantasies about what the dead person looks like can be even more difficult:

'How badly injured was she?'

Rituals provide the background for events which allow children to give direct expression to their feelings. By putting drawings, letters, objects or flowers in or on the coffin, by being able to talk to the dead person, by following the coffin to the grave and so on, concrete and direct expression of inner feelings is encouraged, expression which may be difficult to achieve in any other way. Children usually express themselves more through actions and play than through words, and ritual actions can give direct expression to subconscious and conscious feelings. At the same time, rituals consist of a clear beginning and end, so that the feelings are easier to deal with.

Rituals also give adults and children a common starting point for discussion about the death, not only in the subsequent weeks, but also later in the child's life.

Taken together, rituals promote an understanding of what has happened at the same time as they facilitate emotional expression of grief. Rituals are important for a grieving child in the adjustment to a new 'inner' life where the longing has to be lived with cognitively and emotionally, and in the adaptation to activities where the dead person no longer will take part. Through rituals a child translates thoughts and feelings to concrete symbolic acts.

Viewing the dead body
Preparation for viewing the dead body
In Norway, it has become fairly usual for children to see the dead person on one of the first days following the death, before the funeral. Around an open coffin family members and close friends can say their goodbyes. Most funeral services are held in church, even for non-religious people, and the majority of people are buried. In other countries and cultures, practices vary enormously, but the principles of listening to children, explaining to them and involving them remain the best advice to be given.

Before children are taken to see the dead person, they must be prepared for this situation. This is, of course, particularly the case with the 'older' young children. Being prepared means having been informed about:

- what the room looks like, including the way it has been decorated, for example with flowers, paintings, candles and so on

- what the coffin looks like, the fact that it is open, what colour it is, how it is decorated, carved and so forth

- what the dead person looks like, the colour of their face and hands, and if the death was due to an accident, suicide or murder, what injuries can be seen and which have been covered up. Someone who knows the dead person well should go in first and then tell the child in which ways the dead person looks different

- the temperature in the room, that the dead person has been kept cool and therefore feels cold on touch, that the outer layer of the skin feels soft, but can feel hard under the soft skin

- that it does not matter if the adults react by crying a great deal and get very upset, that this is because they loved the dead person so much

- that they are allowed to react just as they feel, and nobody will mind if they do not cry. If they feel like crying, that is fine. They should know that they can touch, hug or kiss the dead person if they want, but that it is OK if they do not want to, but they might see adults do this

Young children are not always patient enough to keep quiet and stay still for a long time in a situation like this. Children are curious and can investigate the room and the dead person more than adults think appropriate, for example they may stick their finger in the mouth or nose of the dead person or try to open his or her eyes. When adults are prepared for and allow children's 'research' needs, this eases the situation. Children may need to be taken out after a while or should be allowed to move around and play a little in the room.

It may be advisable that someone who knew the deceased well enters the room alone first to look at the room and the dead person before returning to those who are waiting and giving a detailed account of what is awaiting them. If the hair is combed in a different manner from usual, they should make a special effort to inform the child before entering.

The reason so much emphasis has been put on preparation for the viewing is because this reduces the likelihood of the situation being 'etched' on to the child's mind in the form of a traumatic memory. A child who has been poorly prepared can, in the worst case, experience negative, traumatic images being etched in detail and deeply into their memory. If the child has been well prepared, she will be able to recognize the situation:

'It's just like you said, Daddy!'

We also know that children may have strong opinions about what clothes the dead person should wear in the coffin, and adults can involve children in this decision: 'I want her to wear the dress she had on on my birthday!'

If the death takes place at home after a long illness, it may be natural for the dead person to be prepared and laid out at home until the funeral, and that the symbolic ceremony takes place there. Children will often form their own small ceremonies in this kind of situation:

Five-year old Grete's little brother died at home after a long illness. Afterwards he lay in the room for 24 hours. His father put him in the coffin. Members of the family came and went and said their goodbyes. Grete said goodbye her own way. She stayed in her brother's room, sang and 'read' for him and talked to him. She fetched a special flower from the sitting room and put it by his head, then she put a coin in his hand, and finally made sure he had a little car and his teddy with him.

The viewing

The child should be accompanied by a close person whom they trust, when they go to see the dead person. If his mother, father, sister or brother has died, the parents or the surviving parent will themselves be in shock and grief, and they may need to see the dead person first so that they have the chance to react freely without needing to pull themselves together for the child's sake. Afterwards, they can take the child in, or another close person can do so, explaining what is going on, giving the support the child needs, or take the child out if they have had enough. It is particularly important to make the adults' reactions comprehensible to children if they witness strong reactions from them.

Children who are present at the ceremony must be allowed to give concrete expression to their grief. This means that they have made or brought something to put in or on the dead person's coffin. This ritual action has great symbolic force and is important in the child's process of grief. Children only need to be given the idea of taking something they can put in or on the coffin; they will often have a number of concrete thoughts about what that should be. The sort of objects or things they can take are a drawing, a letter, a poem, a CD, a book, photographs, a message read into a cassette, hand-picked or other flowers or other objects with symbolic value, for example something they have made for Mummy or Daddy in their kindergarten. They should put what they have brought into or on the coffin themselves, or into the dead person's hands; this is the most concrete way of saying farewell. Sometimes they may not be able to do this themselves and others have to assist.

If the death happened suddenly, and there was no opportunity to say goodbye before the person died, then it is possible to say goodbye at this gathering. This can be done by saying something aloud or inside, or by whispering something in the dead person's ear. Young children learn through their senses. Some children go right up to the dead person and touch them – hands and hair are particularly important in this context – whereas others are more cautious. This should be treated with tact; the child should not be pressured but should also be told that it is allowed to touch or kiss the dead person. If they do not want to, they should be told that there are other children who do not want to either. Younger children who see a dead person in the coffin need to be told that the lid is put on before the coffin is buried. This is because their concrete way of thinking leads them to believe that the dead person will get earth on them: 'It must be horrible for Mummy getting earth in her mouth down in the grave.'

If a child does not want to see the dead person, you should spend some time outside, supporting and motivating them to do so, but do not exert any pressure. Some children leave very quickly, but may want to return later. Let the child set the pace.

It has also become more usual to take photographs of the dead person in the coffin. Children have a less inhibited relationship to these pictures than adults. They may ask to see them, and want to show them to their friends and relations. Here also we must be careful about allowing adult barriers to inhibit children's natural needs. If pictures or video film have been taken of a dead child, these may be useful when children born later become interested in their brother or sister who died, usually around the age of four to six. Such pictures can become an important support for a child's memory as time goes by, because the memory of preschool children needs outer links and adult conversation to be maintained. It can be especially important for a child coming into the teenage years to have been present at a viewing and then it may be good to keep any pictures.

After the viewing

Even if the ceremony takes place after careful preparation, and with adult support, it can be a very strong experience for a child. The child must, therefore, have the opportunity to ask questions straight away, and to sit down with the adults and be able to talk about what they have all just been through. It may take some time before questions and thoughts present themselves, and children should have the opportunity to express what they have experienced for some time afterwards. They need to confirm their experiences. Young children who have had their first concrete meeting with death may say: 'Now I can't have my bath with Daddy any more. Now we can't go for walks together any more.' This shows that the child is gathering these impressions into a new understanding of what death is. On other occasions, they may have a lot of questions or they may ask to visit the dead person again.

After the viewing the child can be informed about what happens to the body in the time before the burial/cremation, that is, that he or she will stay in the coffin in a room at the hospital or the chapel and is then brought to the church or cremation place before the funeral takes place.

Preschool children can re-enact rituals in detail after the death, when they are playing:

Five-year-old Martha used the sandpit to act out her older sister's funeral. She repeatedly buried a toy lion. She put a cross on the grave, laid toy flowers on it and invited adults and children to come and visit the grave. The repetition of these rituals helped her to integrate the events she had taken part in and gave her new opportunities to express her thoughts and feelings.

When should a child not participate?

Children should not view the dead person in situations where he or she has been injured beyond recognition. This is, for example, the case when the person has died in a fire and is very charred. Lesser burns, for example when the outer skin has been burnt and looks red, should not lead to the child being excluded. The dead person can be prepared so that a viewing is possible. Some aeroplane and explosion accidents also mean that a viewing is impossible because the dead person's body has been too severely damaged. Other ritual ceremonies can be used in situations like these. However, in cases where the dead person's body has been found a long time after the death and has partly disintegrated, such as if the body has been in the sea or on land, it would also be inadvisable to have it shown. Normally a dead person can be shown after road traffic accidents, accidents at work and so forth despite extensive injuries.

Sometimes parts of the dead person have to be covered up with bandages or in another way. It is not unusual for surviving children and adults to comment that 'Those are his hands. Now I know it's him.' Many adults will worry about taking children with them if the dead person has been injured. Remember that children have as much right as the adults to be there. They will never have the chance again, and if they are prepared for the situation, they will react naturally and without drama. It is we adults who set up mental barriers for children's participation. Children experience these situations as concrete and natural.

Supposing the child is against it?

A child should never be pressured into taking part. If the child is strongly against taking part, you can try to motivate them: 'It's important that you come, because this is the last time you'll see Daddy. Later, when you're older, you'll think it was important that you came. I'll be there all the time, and you don't have to be there for long if you don't want to.' If the child is frightened about what they are going to see, you can say: 'I know you're worried about what she looks like, as she was so badly hurt that she died from her injuries. I shall go in first, and then I'll come and tell you what she looks like.' It is unusual for preschool children not to want to see the dead person as long as their parents do not dramatize things. If they are in doubt, you can say: 'You don't need to decide this right now. Think about it, and we'll talk about it later.' It is often possible for children to have a look a day later than planned if they change their mind.

You can also tell your child that they will be thoroughly prepared for what they will see, and that other children who at first did not want to go to a viewing have later said that they were very glad that they did.

Supposing the parents are against it?

If the parents are absolutely unable to think of taking their children with them, healthcare workers or a priest should ensure that they understand how important it is that the children can be present, and the injustice we can do to children if we exclude them. When parents are in doubt, it is important that they have time to let these thoughts sink in. The reasons parents do not want their children to take part are usually:

- They think it will be harmful for the child.

- Other people have said they should not bring the child.

- They are frightened of the situation themselves, of how they will react and how their reactions may affect the child.

All experience shows that children who are well prepared for a viewing and are accompanied by an adult who can give them support will not be harmed by it. The advice not to take the child is usually based on the erroneous and simplified belief that it is better for the child to remember the dead person as he or she was, which does not take into account the long-term significance that participation in a viewing can have for preventing fantasies and making the death real.

Children who participate in a viewing do not have more difficulties remembering the dead person as he or she was in life. The child's choice is often made by her parents, but it is the child who will have to live on without having had the chance to take part in an important family event.

Some children, regardless of a good preparation, can struggle with memories from the viewing. They can see the dead person in front of them at bedtime or have nightmares where they see the dead person as he or she looked in the coffin. If the child starts having problems falling or staying asleep, it is important to ask them if they are seeing such images. Modern psychological therapy methods can usually quickly reduce such problems.

When children get older they may blame the adults for not letting them join in. If the parents do not wish their children to attend a viewing, they should spend some time thinking about this. If the parents know that the priest, the undertakers or healthcare workers will be there and support them through the ritual, it will be easier for them to take their children. If they still feel unable to let their children attend, it is important that they can tell them about it afterwards in as much detail as possible, so that the children's fantasies will be counteracted, and they will gain a better understanding of what happened during the ritual.

Should very young children take part in these rituals?

Young age should not be a reason for not taking children to a viewing. A very young child of less than three years will not understand very much of what is happening, but the fact that he has taken part will have great symbolic significance for him when he is older. This argument is, of course, only relevant if it is a close relative of the child who has died, like his mother, father, a sibling or grandparent:

> Karl, who is 16 years old, says he wishes he had been to see his dead father and had taken part in the funeral at the time of his father's death when he was one year old. 'It would have been so good to know that my mother had carried me in to see Dad, and that I'd been there.'

The preparations must, however, be adapted to the child's age. The very youngest children will not understand what is happening and will have to be carried securely in someone's arms.

The funeral, cremation, memorials and later rituals

Much of what has just been discussed is also true for the funeral. Children should be well prepared, have a close, trusted adult by their side whom they can question and express their thoughts and reactions to after the ceremony.

Ritual actions can be important for the child at the funeral also, in the form of a flower, a drawing and so on, which they can put on the coffin. Children who have lost a sibling may want to tell a little story or rhyme their brother or sister was particularly fond of, or sing the goodnight song they liked so much. This should not be pressured, but the opportunity should be there.

The priest or person speaking should make his memorial words about the dead person simple, so that children can understand as much as possible, and should also include important experiences that the deceased and the surviving child shared. The person can reduce the adults' anxiety that the child will 'spoil' the ceremony of the occasion by saying how positive and important it is that children are included and that it does not matter if they make some noise in the chapel.

Older preschool children should be given the opportunity to take part in the gathering after the funeral where memories and episodes connected to the deceased are brought to life: memories which may be important for the child's understanding and respect for the deceased. However, young children cannot be expected to behave formally and sit still throughout the whole of this memorial gathering. Children must be allowed to be children and should not be told off all the time because they are making a noise or are not showing enough respect.

Ritual ceremonies can later be connected to special days and holidays. These rituals may channel religious feelings, and they may serve as concrete connections to the feelings of loss, longing and grief. Many children share the belief that they will meet the dead person again in the afterlife, even if they do not find comfort in other aspects of religion. Through ritual ceremonies, feelings can be expressed directly through action, and bridges can be built over the loss.

Ceremony and help in the kindergarten

If a child in the kindergarten dies, preschool children need an explanation of what has happened in a simple language adjusted to their age. If there is time to inform parents, it is very safe for children to sit on their lap while what happened and why is explained. Owing to their lack of experience and concept development we need to be sure that children have understood what is being said in order to reduce misunderstandings. Safe surroundings with physical closeness is very important for young children, together with good advice to parents about how they can follow up the event at home. Parents should expect and allow more clinginess and temporary sleeping in the parents' room; they should keep up ordinary routines and so on. It can be said to children that sometimes we become sad, angry or afraid after someone dies. If that happens they can seek out Mama or Papa or one of the adults in the kindergarten to get some comfort and talk with him or her about their feelings. If they start thinking thoughts that make them sad or angry they can also let more happy, good or 'strong' thoughts take away the other thoughts. Strong thoughts are those like: 'Mama or Papa is here and will console me', 'I will think about something nice', or they can think of their favourite cartoon.

Close friends from the kindergarten can also be taken to the funeral of a child, but they should be accompanied by their parents and staff from the kindergarten so that they are with trusted and close people who care for them. In some cases these children may be quite lost in this kind of ceremony, especially if there has been an event which has devastated a whole community so that the church is full. If this is the case, it could be arranged for the group of children to come up to the coffin beforehand (an hour before, for example), so that they can say goodbye in person and without being disturbed.

Rituals can also be used in the kindergarten. A memorial gathering could, for example, consist of the following:

- gathering the children together
- lighting candles, perhaps with flowers, next to a picture of the dead child
- a few words from the preschool teacher about the child who has died
- songs or music.

Candles could also be lit on special days following the death and up to the end of the Christmas or summer term (for example, on the child's birthday).

The children in the kindergarten can also be involved in packing up the things the dead child has left behind in the kindergarten. This must be done with the understanding of the child's parents. The children could also draw a picture for the child's parents, and these drawings could be given together with the personal effects which are to be returned. A candle could be lit next to a picture of the child up to the time of the funeral. After the ritual, the picture should be put out for the end of term performance and party.

No matter what has happened, the children should be told about the death. This should be done in a calm, concrete and direct way. As many children invent their own concepts of cause and chain of events, it is important to listen to the questions children ask and the discussions they have, so that any misconceptions can be explained and fantasies can be reduced. If the children have taken part in the funeral, this could well be the theme for play and drawing for a while, as children process events naturally in this way. There may be many direct questions or comments:

'Could I get ill and die like Morten?'

'I don't want to get dead.'

'He'll come back after Christmas, won't he?'

It is often necessary to talk about what has happened for a long time afterwards. It can be very useful to use books about loss and grief during this period. At the end of this book, there is a list of books which deal with the experience of loss for children in different ways, whether this is as a result of death, divorce or other causes.

Follow-up in the kindergarten

A kindergarten should have an emergency plan that details the procedures to be followed in the event of a death, but also for deaths that happen away from the kindergarten or other deaths that affect or make a strong impression on several children, including events which attract wide media coverage. By making crises and death a theme for a planning day, by preparing an action plan and by planning who does what and when, the kindergarten will be better prepared if the worst should happen. More information about such planning can be found in the 'Resources' at the end of this book.

Parents should be present when an incident of death that took place in the kindergarten, or that all the children have been deeply affected by, is to be reviewed. The children can sit in a circle on their parents' laps while events are talked about. This gives the sense of security needed to be able to talk about such painful things, as well as a shoulder to cry on if needed. The death should be gone through in a concrete way, using words the children understand, and carefully stimulating the children to relate what happened or what they have understood. Drawings, glove puppets and so on may also be used to bring out spontaneous expression from the children. The adults may need to repeat the facts and at the same time ensure that these young children have understood what has happened. Young children do not have fully developed verbal skills to express different sides of the event, but they can be encouraged by listening to what other children say and by support from the adults.

The information that can be given about the usual reactions in this group is limited, but they may be helped by some simple, concrete pieces of advice if they have sad or difficult thoughts:

- Talk to Mummy or Daddy about it.

- Let happy thoughts come and push the other ones away.

- Make a trap to trick the bad thoughts.

Young children have a small repertoire of mastery and therefore need simple pieces of advice on what to do. Sometimes they can think of ideas more easily if you say: 'What can we do when we get difficult thoughts about what has happened?' Sometimes you can get a rush of suggestions from young children when they get the chance to use their imagination.

Chapter Four

How do children process what has happened over time?

———◆———

Children have a great need to be reminded of the person who is no longer there, and at the same time to process what has happened. They can be helped with this in different ways.

Keep children in touch with concrete memories

Children look at pictures of the person who is no longer there. There may be periods when they do this every day, and they may at the same time choose a toy they associate with the dead or lost person, which they carry around with them and which they want to have in their bed when they sleep. This can be seen in even very young children.

If there is a grave, the children want to visit the grave. If the cemetery is close to the child's home, they can visit the grave alone from about the age of seven. After an accident a child may find it helpful to 'inspect' the scene to take in what happened. In some cases this is when children first under-stand what has happened. They may also want to visit places they have been with the deceased. Even though it may be dif-ficult for parents to do things like this with their children, it will be a great help for them.

Let children ask questions

Children grasp and process what has happened through the answers their parents give to their questions. Parents relate that they are asked a lot of questions about the dead person and about death:

'Did the baby have to climb all the way to heaven?'

'Is it cold down in the grave?'

It is through asking these constant and rather detailed questions that children increase their ability to understand and master what has happened. The direct and sometimes brutal questions may be both painful and difficult to answer, but parents must answer truthfully, and they must admit to what they do not know. If children are mature enough to ask a question, they are mature enough to hear the answer. Some children's questions are very direct and their comments can be unexpected, painful and surprising:

'He does not need the tools any more – I am the man in the house now!'

'I have told Steve that they can have the baby carriage because we do not need it any longer and he will soon get a baby brother.'

If comments or questions are painful and we need time to think before responding, we could say: 'This is too painful for Mama to talk about right now and therefore I am a little sad and cry a little. That is OK and I promise you that we shall talk more about this later.'

Although some children will need to hear the chain of events repeated over and over again in order to understand what has happened and to counteract misunderstandings, others, even very young children, can be unwilling to talk about what has happened. It is too painful and they may need some time before they are able to talk about the loss. If a child is otherwise acting normally in the kindergarten and/or at home and they are getting on well with their peers, there is no particular cause for concern. This reaction reflects the way children regulate the strong feelings they have. They will gradually open up and will set the pace themselves.

Play helps children to understand better

Many children carry out funeral rituals where they bury animals and insects. This is both helpful and supportive for them as they try to understand what has happened to the dead person. They may also make drawings of graves with crosses, or of other situations associated with death or loss. This is the natural way for children to express themselves and it helps them to grasp what has happened. Parents should not try to stop play of this kind.

Having coloured pencils or pens readily available for children may encourage them to draw what has happened, or the fantasies, thoughts and feelings they have. Many children from the age of three to four years are able to express thoughts and feelings in this way. But parents can also provide support for children by getting involved in role-play or play-acting which a child is directing, for example when a child is testing out what death is by pulling the bed covers over his head and saying: 'Now I am dead.'

If a child was present at a dramatic death, you could try to have toys available which can be used to recreate what happened, for example a boat if it was a boat accident or an ambulance if the child was present when the ambulance came for the person in the accident, and so on.

You could also make a memorial album with the child, where pictures and drawings and other things the child has made are stuck in. Newspaper cuttings and other things the child associates with the person who is no longer there can be kept in a special box, which the child can fetch and look at when they want to.

Music is another important means to help children express feelings and thoughts. Playing music or singing songs children associate with the person who has died can bring forth tears and the loss is allowed to rise up and be given joint expression. Talking about loss is often better with music in the background. Sometimes music can release the lump a child is carrying inside himself.

Children can protect adults

Children pick up at an early stage what they can talk about and what they should not ask or bring up. They can see when Mummy or Daddy are sad and they realize when their parents have had a bad day. In the first instance, they avoid talking about the loss so as not to cause additional pain. In the second instance they come and comfort and give support: 'Don't be sad, Mummy, you've still got me.'

Some children become very upset from seeing that their parents are sad. A five-year-old asked his mother to pull up the corners of her mouth and show her teeth, saying: 'You don't need to smile, but you can pretend to.'

It is not easy to deal with reactions like these. Adults must be allowed to show their feelings, and mourning adults cannot be expected to put their face into a smiling mask all the time. The child's disquiet may be lessened if adults put words to their reactions, and explain that grown-ups feel sad even more when someone they love is no longer there, while children are involved with other things which means that they can forget their sadness for a while. Meanwhile, the child needs to be told that Mummy and/or Daddy will gradually become less sad, and although they are feeling sad, they will always be there for them.

Provide closeness and physical contact

Young children need closeness and physical contact to feel secure. When Mummy or Daddy is carrying them, they feel themselves being rocked and cradled, and the touch of their hands and tone of voice confirms the feeling of closeness and security. Changes in the rhythm and intonation of the voice, a different facial expression with less smiling than usual and less time for cuddles and care are picked up as signals that something has happened. A loss, especially when dramatic and sudden, often results in parents giving their children less physical contact. This can give children a feeling of insecurity and can make them restless, complaining and clinging, which can lead to a vicious circle. So it is important that parents maintain physical contact in these situations. If the child has been present at a dramatic event in connection with the loss, careful stoking, patting and simple 'body massage' will help to calm them and will help prevent them from developing problems over time.

Keeping up physical contact will signal continuity and security in the child's everyday life, in addition to the fact that it is believed to have a directly soothing effect on the tension the child may be feeling. Amazingly, mothers who massage their children will also reduce their own anxiety and depression.

Chapter Five

Supporting children over time

Children continue processing a major loss over time. As they grow older and more mature, they will have new questions to ask. They may become interested in other aspects of the loss: 'Was it because Daddy didn't love me that he didn't want to live here any more?', 'Do you think Mummy died because I didn't tidy my room?' Adults need to listen out for changes in the child's way of thinking and to be willing to follow them in their philosophical thoughts about how things are. Children gradually develop a greater capacity for thinking in more complex ways, and some may create rescue fantasies where they rework what has happened in their thoughts, sometimes with themselves as heroes, preventing the loss. Masterful thoughts like these are usually a good sign, but with the increasing ability to imagine the chain of events differently, children may also become more judgemental towards themselves: 'If only I hadn't shouted to Daddy, the accident wouldn't have happened.' Thoughts like these are more common in schoolchildren, but some preschool children can also juggle with such thoughts. Sensitive adults who are open to these thoughts, and do not just say 'You mustn't think like that' straight away, can help children to gain control over and overcome this kind of self-blame.

Preschool children may suddenly be filled with loss and longing, and can think about the person who is no longer there for a long time after the loss. Sometimes they want confirmation that adults are thinking about that person too:

> Jørgen was four and a half years old when his father died. About one year later he looks at his mother, waits a moment, then asks cautiously: 'Do you think about Daddy when you open a door?'

This shows the way he thinks of his daddy and misses him in completely everyday situations. As his mother did not mention him so often, he wanted to know whether she also thought about his father a great deal.

Children who lose someone early in life, often take longer to build up an existential sense of security. For children who have lost someone dear to them early in life, it is not a matter of course that those they love will always be around them. As their concepts of the world, what it is like and what can happen in it, develop, there will be space for much disquiet and anxiety. If, in addition to the loss of a parent through death or divorce, children also experience other changes in their life, such as moving, changing kindergarten or the appearance of a new person who is going to look after them when their mother or father is at work, this insecurity can be intensified. Stability in the child's everyday life contributes to an increased sense of security. The child may also need reassurances that the remaining parents are still there and will stay with them: 'Mummy isn't ill. Mummy isn't going to die; she'll always be with you.'

Loss can have an effect on children's development and can make them vulnerable to later losses, or can lead to their inner 'models' or presumptions about the world around them being different from those of other children. Caring and understanding adults in the home, in the kindergarten and at school reduce the chances of children developing in an unbalanced way. Looking back later in life, it is difficult to remember things that happened before the age of five years. This puts a particular responsibility on us as adults to help these children to maintain an inner image and relationship with the person who is no longer there. Only by talking about the lost person, looking at pictures, video films and so on, is it possible for children to keep an inner image. They need this image to continue processing what has happened over the years to come.

In families with an open style of communication where children experience a safe environment with room for their questions, thoughts and feelings, they can gradually achieve new understanding of what happened with increasing age. Conversations about the death over time must leave room for children's gradual understanding and development of their own narrative, parallel with adults helping them fill in this story. When parents manage to sustain such an elaborative interactive communication over time, children both gain a better understanding of what happened and better emotional regulation than where conversations seldom occur or are more restrictive. In fact it is through conversations where parents together with their child or children reminisce about previous events, such as the loss of a loved one, that children's verbal, cognitive and emotional development is stimulated.

Whilst it was thought a few decades ago that it was important for children to forget, we have now learnt that the inner image a child has of the person who died is important for them later, when there will be periods when they are very interested in the mother, father or sibling who is no longer there. It is easier for children to keep their good memories when adults talk to them about the person who is no longer there, not just in the first period after a loss, but also over a long time.

Advice to parents

When children experience grief, their parents are also going through a difficult period. Many parents can find that their ability to take care of their children is reduced for a while. This may lead to them:

- being less aware of their child's needs
- having difficulties maintaining rules and discipline and being more lenient with their children
- being more irritable and bad-tempered
- being more overprotective and cautious.

Many parents struggle with guilty feelings about the way they have been treating their children:

> A mother and her two children experienced a dramatic death in the mother's family. Things went well for the first weeks, but during the course of the first six months, the mother became more and more depressed in addition to the fact that she blamed herself for what had happened. Therapy helped the mother to get her feelings of guilt under control and she became less depressed. As she got her own problems under control, she became overwhelmingly guilty about her two preschool children: 'I haven't been able to take care of them. I have been so bad-tempered and cross. How awful it must have been for them.' One of the children in particular had been severely traumatized from having been present at the death, and later needed help from a psychologist. The help to the mother consisted of recognition of the fact that she was exhausted, that she had done her best and that she could learn from this. Meanwhile her self-reproach was greater than it needed to have been, so that going over everything she had in fact done for her children helped her to gain a more realistic evaluation of the situation.

When young children lose a parent, the remaining parent has lost a partner. For many this will lead to long-term, not seldom complicated, grief reactions. This can temporarily or permanently reduce parental capacity and the fine-tuned interplay between a child and its parent can be disturbed. In later years our knowledge about the consequences of depression in parents, especially mothers, has increased greatly. If parents' mood is lowered over time it can lead to different problems in the interplay between parents and children, which eventually will influence the child negatively, both regarding behavioural problems and withdrawing from others. It is within their interaction with parents that children gradually learn to regulate their emotions. When a mother or father consoles, soothes, calms down, explains and reassures, children gradually develop the ability to do this themselves. If a mother and/or father have experienced a painful loss they may become temporarily unable to be as sensitive to their children's needs as before, and the children may have their emotional regulation learning disturbed. Girls seem to be more influenced by reduced parental capacity in their mothers than boys.

It is almost inevitable and fully understandable that a remaining parent will have less energy for their children after their partner's death. In situations where parental capacity is temporarily reduced other caretakers or adults can be very important in the children's life. Good support for children is best promoted by the parents being able to process what has happened. In addition they should also seek information and advice about their children's needs, children's usual reactions and how they can support and help their children. Staff from the health service and kindergartens can give advice on how children should be cared for after a loss. If parents can get help to alleviate painful memories, irritability, fatigue or depression, they will have more energy to take care of their children.

Participation in groups for adults after a divorce or loss through death can play an important part in helping parents to cope better. It is particularly important to ensure openness and directness in the inner communication of the family, so that new facts about the loss can be passed on to the children and no difficulties or breakdown in confidence occur in the interaction between children and their parents.

When parents divorce, they must each avoid criticizing the other when they are together with the child, so that the child does not end up in an awkward position between the two. If a child has to listen to negative characterizations of one of her parents from the other, her inner picture of her mother and/or father will easily become confused. Children who experience this also develop a lesser belief in themselves (a weakened self-image). Discontent with the other party must be dealt with at an adult level, without the child being made a messenger of negative messages or reproaches, or a discussion partner or comforter for the parent. The better and the closer the relationship between the child and the parent who is no longer living with her on a daily basis, the less the negative effects of the divorce will be for the child. One of the most important things parents can do after a divorce is to build the best possible relationship with each other. This helps to prevent children being afraid for the future, or feeling anxious or frustrated with life.

If the parents are really exhausted, other caring people can be a good support for the children. If the parents can accept that they do not have enough energy for their children for a period, it is easier for them to understand that other adults whom the children trust can be useful people who can give them support for a period after the loss. There is a great difference between not having enough energy for our children for a while, and ignoring this fact.

If a child in the family dies, it can lead to high anxiety in parents that something else will happen. Anxious parents induce anxiousness in their children and appropriate help to parents to alleviate anxiety is a good investment for children in the family as well.

If a child has died, it is important that the parents get help to prevent them becoming overprotective and extremely anxious for their other children. Talking about these fears, being aware of them and simple pieces of advice which help to counteract them can prevent these fears having an effect on the other children's development of independence and from limiting their life experiences unnecessarily. Some examples of simple pieces of advice are:

- Train yourself gradually to let your children go from you.

- Watch out for the safety of your child in a way that the child does not notice (e.g. by looking out of an upstairs window).

- Reassure yourself with calming words like: 'Nothing is going to happen to him', 'Other children are all right'.

- Use simple relaxation techniques like those taught at ante-natal classes.

- Avoid reports which reinforce your anxiety, for example reports about other children who have been injured or have died.

Chapter Six

Advice to parents

——◆——

Below is some advice that may help parents to support their children in the grief they are experiencing. It must be emphasized most strongly that this advice must be adapted to the individual situation.

- Make it quite clear to children that they are free to react. If children are uncertain how their reactions may be met by adults, they may hold back. It may therefore be a good idea for adults to say that it does not matter when children or adults become sad or angry when someone dies or parents are getting divorced, and they do not need to hold back their reactions because they are afraid of being laughed at, or of making the adults sad.

- Help children to recognize their reactions and understand what has happened. This does not mean that you should tear down the need children may have to take in the loss little by little, but do not enter into a joint denial of what has happened.

- Say that you will be there in the future. It is important for children to have such reassurances,

because they are often afraid that their parents or
the remaining parent will also leave them.

- By keeping the daily routines as constant as
  possible, continuity and safety are established. This
  will reduce the insecurity and anxiety that children
  might experience. Although a child might protest
  on delivery to the kindergarten, an early return will
  signal that important parts of their daily world
  remains constant. By continuing daily routines of
  meals and bedtime more signals of continuity and
  stability are given to children.

- We adults must listen for underlying themes and
  deeper meaning in children's comments, questions
  and behaviour. Children actively seek frameworks
  of understanding, which they can use to grasp what
  has happened. They must re-shape assumptions
  about the world, other people and themselves, and
  even very young children may have many deep
  thoughts about different aspects of existence.

- We adults can tell children that the thoughts,
  feelings, wishes, behaviour and experiences they
  have are normal. The strong and often unfamiliar
  reactions children experience can be frightening
  because they do not have any earlier experiences as
  a basis of comparison to help them to understand
  them. Even when children keep such thoughts and
  feelings to themselves, or are not old enough to
  formulate them, it can be important for adults to
  put into words the usual thoughts and feelings in a
  situation like this, so that the children understand
  what is going on within them.

- Help young children to recognize, name and
  differentiate between feelings. Tragic situations can

give children such strong experiences that their feelings may be pushed right away or seem to be a whirlwind of powerful reactions they have no control over. Whilst adults have developed the ability to distinguish between feelings, children need an adult's help to put words to, to understand and to differentiate these feelings.

- Traumatic losses make it difficult to regulate the strength of reaction, which may mean that children either try to avoid these strong feelings or they feel completely overwhelmed by them. It is a great help if parents help children to put words to these feelings or express them in another way, and regulate the strength of these reactions.

The list below conveys a summary of good advice.

Open, truthful communication:

- Do not wait to tell the child about the loss. Give precise information about what has happened.

- Say that the dead person will never come back.

- Tell about the viewing of the body and the cremation or funeral.

- In the case of divorce – explain why and what it will be like.

Avoid confusion:

- Do not talk about travelling or sleep. Give exact information about what has happened.

- Avoid abstract explanations.

- Give explanations which are suitable for the child's age.

- In the case of divorce – do not paraphrase what is going on, do not give false hopes.

Allow time for thoughts to be mastered:

- Take time to talk with the child about all that is difficult.

- Questions from the child must be answered, even if they have asked the same thing many times before.

- Go through the chain of events with the child several times.

- Listen to children's thoughts and interpretations about what has happened/is happening.

- Let children draw and play about what has happened or is happening, so that they can express what they are feeling in their own 'language'.

Make the loss real:

- Let children see the dead person, but with good preparation.

- Let children take part in the funeral.

- Do not hide your thoughts and feelings for children.

- Keep reminders in view, make an album, look at pictures and video films.

- Take children to visit the cemetery or the garden of remembrance.

- Grief, loss and longing are natural reactions in children. Let them feel that they can show these feelings.

- In the case of divorce – let children see their 'new home' where they will be spending time with their father or mother at an early stage.

Continuity in the home, school and kindergarten:

- Avoid situations where children have to be separated from their parents, for example by having to stay with their grandparents or others; even short separations can create anxiety.

- Try to keep to the normal routines at home.

- Accept the fact that children may have an increased need for closeness and security.

- Let children go back to kindergarten or school soon afterwards.

- In the case of divorce, children will feel reassured by having familiar things with them (teddy, duvet, dummies, and so on) and this will ease the transition to a new situation.

- In the case of divorce – establish set routines for spending time with each parent as soon as possible.

Children's anxiety that they or their parents will die or go away should be alleviated:

- Talk with children about the fear they are feeling. Give reassurances that their parents will be there and that death or loss happens very seldom.

Relieve any feelings of guilt:

- Let the children put into words, play or draw what they are thinking.

- Reassure children that nothing they have thought or done caused what happened.

When do children need extra help?

If a child's behaviour undergoes a dramatic change that continues over many weeks, that is, isolating totally from friends, becoming quite unmanageable or continuing to complain about bodily symptoms, it can be helpful to seek out professional advice. If the child was present and witnessed or survived a dramatic incidence of death, or was witness to violent episodes in connection with a divorce, we should pay close attention to whether the reactions continue. If children still react after four to five weeks in a way that indicates they are troubled by memories and thoughts (nightmares, sleep disturbances, restlessness and excessive activity, for example), withdraw from others, avoid anything that may remind them of what has happened, or show reactions which indicate an almost constant sense of danger (they are always on guard, are excitable, irritable and so on), then professional help should be sought.

If several risk factors are present and children's behaviour changes remarkably, or strong feelings continue with the same intensity, a child psychologist or child psychiatrist should be contacted for advice on how the processing of their grief can be further supported.

Chapter Seven

Specific advice

———◆———

Below are some simple pieces of advice which can be followed if children show reactions which continue for longer than the first weeks after the loss. If the reactions are strong and lasting, and these pieces of advice do not help, you are recommended to seek professional help.

Increased anxiety:

- stability in the home

- set routines

- reassurances that you are nearby

- physical contact, massage.

Lack of understanding:

- Explain in a concrete way.

- Accept that they will repeatedly ask similar questions.

- Use drawings about the loss, take children to rituals, give them facts.

Confusion:

- Give repeated explanations, use books as support when explaining.

Anxiety about every separation:

- Set routines which are carefully followed.

- Reassure children that you will fetch them from kindergarten.

More childish behaviour:

- Expect this for a while.

- Gradually demand that children manage things by themselves.

Anger:

- Help children to put words to and direct their reactions.

- Make use of active play.

Sleep disturbances:

- Set bedtimes, the presence of the adult is gradually stepped down, low music.

Nightmares:

- Let children tell and draw in detail what has happened in their dreams.

- Sit by their bed and stroke them gently on the back.

- Help children to change the nightmare in any way they like – give suggestions, for example take a hero into the dream.

- Review the new dream at bedtime; let the child say to themself that tonight if they dream it will be this new dream.

Avoidance reactions:

- cautious, gradual approach to the subjects the child is afraid of
- adult support and consolation
- reassurances, quiet talks and comforting body contact (patting, stroking as you approach the things the child is afraid of).

Restlessness and overactivity:

- physical contact, touch, patting and massage
- rhythmical songs
- quiet times, reading
- telling stories.

Sadness and loss:

- normal reactions which last for short periods over a very long time (many years)
- give comfort and support, confirm the child's experience of loss and longing
- do not say: 'Now you've got to be a big boy/girl and stop crying.'

Chapter Eight

Conclusion

Children grieve in different ways. There are more similarities than dissimilarities between adults' and children's grief. The same loss and longings, the same 'strange' thoughts and powerful emotions which are found in adults can be experienced by children who have lost someone they love. However, children's reactions depend to a great degree on the way we, as adults, are able to respond, and the foundation we give them for processing their feelings and reactions.

By letting children take part in rituals for grief, by keeping communication channels open and truthful, and by talking with children about what has happened, the best basis is laid for them to process their feelings and reactions. This puts a heavy responsibility on parents who are grieving themselves. But this also makes the basis for a future close and secure sense of togetherness in the family. In the book *Grief in Children* I have described children's grief at different ages more thoroughly.

Resources

Internet websites with information about children, adolescents and families in grief

- The Compassionate Friends: an organization offering support and encouragement to others after the death of a child.
  (www.tcf.org.uk/leaflets/lesurviving.html)

- Roadcare: a website to help people who have been bereaved as a result of a road traffic accident.
  (www.cadd.org.uk/docs/CADDCoping.pdf)

- The Childhood Bereavement Network is a national federation working with bereaved children and young people.
  (www.childhoodbereavementnetwork.org.uk/haad_about_bereavement_childhood_cr.htm)

- Cruse Bereavement Care: an organization to promote the well-being of bereaved people.
  (www.crusebereavementcare.org.uk)

- Winston's Wish: a charity for bereaved children: helps bereaved children and young people rebuild their lives after a family death. They offer practical support and guidance to families, professionals and anyone concerned about a grieving child.
  (www.winstonswish.org.uk)

- RD4U (Road for You): a website designed for young people by young people. It is part of Cruse Bereavement Care's Youth Involvement Project and is intended to support people after the death of someone close. (www.rd4u.org.uk)

- The Child Bereavement Charity: by listening to bereaved children and parents, The Child Bereavement Charity aims to improve the care offered by professionals to grieving families in the immediate crisis and in the many months following the death of someone important in their lives. (www.childbereavement.org.uk)

- Resources for Children Experiencing Grief: a resource guide created in order to make materials available to adults essential in the lives of children experiencing grief. (www.kidsgrief.com/index.html)

- Growthhouse: a website devoted to helping children and young adults work through grief and serious illness. (www.growthhouse.org/childgrv.html)

Books about loss to read with young children

Goodbye Mousie
Robie H. Harris
Illustrated by Jan Ormerod
Simon & Schuster Children's Books

I Miss You: First Look at Death
Pat Thomas
Barron's Educational Series

When Uncle Bob Died (Talking It Through)
'Althea'
Illustrated by Sarah Wimperis
Happy Cat Books

Bibliography

d'Aquili, E.G., Laughlin, C.D. Jr. and McManus, J. (1979) *The Spectrum of Ritual. A Biogenetic Structural Analysis.* New York, NY: Columbia University Press.

Bøge, P. and Dige, J. (2005) *OmSorg handleplan 0-6 år.* København: Kræftens Bekæmpelse.

Cerel, J., Fristad, M.A., Verducci, J., Weller, R.A. and Weller, E.B. (2006) 'Childhood bereavement: psychopathology in the 2 years postparental death.' *Journal of the American Academy of Child and Adolescent Psychiatry 45*, 681–690.

Dawson, G., Ashman, S.B., Panagiotides, H., Hessl, D., Self, J., Yamada, E. and Embry, L. (2003) 'Preschool outcomes of children with depressed mothers: role of maternal behavior, contextual risk, and children's brain activity.' *Child Development 74*, 1158–1175.

Dyregrov, A. (2008) *Beredskapsplan för skolen.* Bergen: Fagbokforlaget.

Dyregrov, A. (2008) *Grief in Children* (2nd edition). London: Jessica Kingsley Publishers.

Egeberg, M. (1993) 'Ritualenes betydning i lokalsamfunnet.' *Omsorg nr 4*, 34–38.

Feijo, L., Hernandez-Reif, M., Field, T., Burns, W., Valley-Gray, S. and Simco, E. (2006) 'Mothers' depressed mood and anxiety levels are reduced after massaging their preterm infants.' *Infant Behavior & Development 29*, 476–480.

Jacobsen, A. (1989) *Det var en gang vi ikke var her* [There Was Once a Time We Were Not Here]. Copenhagen: Hans Reitzels forlag.

Raundalen, M. (2000) 'Hva skal vi si til barn om selvmord?' *Suicidiologi 5*, 12–15. Text available at: www.krisepsyk.no (accessed on 11 January 2008).

Silk, J.S., Shaw, D.S., Skuban, E.M., Oland, A.A. and Kovacs, M. (2006) 'Emotion regulation strategies in offspring of childhood-onset depressed mothers.' *Journal of Child Psychology and Psychiatry 47*, 69–78.

Silverman, P.R. and Worden, J.W. (1992) 'Children's understanding of funeral ritual.' *Omega 25*, 319–331.

Slaughter, V. (2005) 'Young children's understanding of death.' *Australian Psychologist 40*, 179–186.

Turner, S.M., Beidel, D.C. and Roberson-Nay, R. (2005) 'Offspring of anxious parents: reactivity, habituation, and anxiety-proneness.' *Behaviour Research and Therapy 43*, 1263–1279.

Wareham, P. and Salmon, K. (2006) 'Mother–child reminiscing about everyday experiences: implications for psychological interventions in the preschool years.' *Clinical Psychology Review 26*, 535–554.

Index

GRIEF IN CHILDREN

A HANDBOOK FOR ADULTS

ATLE DYREGROV

Foreword by Professor William Yule

144 pages ISBN 978 1 84310 612 8 pb

Praise for the author:

> 'Dyregrov's writing is clear in its description...explicit in its advice, and demonstrates that the daunting task of helping a child through grief is both manageable and rewarding... The book will, I'm sure, become required reading for all those touched by the care of bereaved children.'
>
> *— Bereavement Care*

> '...a handy, small book ideal for teachers, social workers, counsellors, parents and others faced with the task of understanding children in grief and trying to help them.'
>
> *— Association for Child Psychology and Psychiatry Newsletter*

This fully updated second edition of *Grief in Children* explains children's understanding of death at different ages and provides information on how the adults around them can best help them cope.

Whether a child experiences the death or loss of a friend, family member, classmate or teacher, it is important for those caring for a bereaved child to know how to respond to their needs. Illustrated with case studies and incorporating the latest findings about grief in children, this accessible guide explores the methods of approaching grief that have been shown to work, provides advice on how loss and bereavement should be handled at school, explains when it is appropriate to enlist expert professional help and discusses the value of support for children and caregivers.

This book is essential reading for parents, carers, counsellors, teachers and all those concerned with the welfare of bereaved children.

Contents: Foreword. Introduction. 1. Children's grief and crisis reaction. 2. Different types of death. 3. Death and crisis at different developmental levels. 4. What makes the grief worse? 5. Sex differences in children's grief. 6. Care for children in grief and crisis. 7. Guidelines for taking care of children's needs. 8. Handling death in the play group and at school. 9. Crisis- or grief-therapy for children. 10. Bereavement groups for children. 11. Caring for oneself. Appendix: Grief in children – guidelines for care. Resources. References. Index.

Order this book online now via our website: www.jkp.com.